W9-AJT-533

BRUMBACK LIBRARY
Western outlaws.
Surge, Frank.
920 Su7w
JNF
c1
3 3045 00003 2405

western outlaws

A Pull Ahead Book

western outlaws

Frank Surge

Lerner Publications Company • Minneapolis, Minnesota

DC

ACKNOWLEDGMENTS: The illustrations are reproduced through the courtesy of: p. 6, Kansas State Historical Society; pp. 9, 54, Pinkerton's Inc. Archives; p. 10, State Historical Society of Missouri; pp. 11, 13, 15, 37, National Archives; pp. 17, 22, Wells Fargo Bank, San Francisco; pp. 18, 39, Independent Picture Service; pp. 24, 27, 29, 36, 40, 43, 45, University of Oklahoma Library, N.H. Rose Collection; p. 25, University of Texas Library; pp. 30, 32, 34, Oklahoma Historical Society; pp. 48, 49, Arizona Dept. of Library and Archives; pp. 51, 53, Utah State Historical Society.

 Published simultaneously in Canada by J. M. Dent & Sons, Ltd., Don Mills, Ontario.

Library of Congress Catalog Number: 68-30567

contents

Jesse James 7
Billy the Kid 12
Joaquin Murieta 17
The Reno Brothers 20
Black Bart 23
Sam Bass 24
John Wesley Hardin 27
Belle Starr 31
The Daltons 35
Bill Doolin 38
Bill Cook 42
Cherokee Bill 44
The Apache Kid 48
The Wild Bunch 50

Jesse James

Jesse James

Jesse Woodson James, the most famous of all American outlaws, was born September 5, 1847, in Clay County, Missouri. When he was 16 he rode with Quantrill, leader of a lawless band of raiders in Missouri during the Civil War. After the war he formed his own outlaw band with his older brother Frank, the famous Younger Brothers, and others. Jesse James was 5′11″, solidly built, fair, blue-eyed, and bearded. He was a brave, cruel, violent man, a thief and a killer. Frank James was quieter and more careful. The Younger Brothers—Cole, Jim, Bob, and John—were big, good-humored men. They were also thieves and killers.

In a 16-year period the James gang pulled off 17 bank and train robberies. They took in $200,000 in loot. The gang was small and tightly-knit. Their robberies were carefully planned, the scenes thoroughly scouted in advance. Jesse's most persistent enemies were Allan Pinkerton and his son William, founders of the famous Pinkerton Detective Agency.

On April 24, 1875, Jesse married his first cousin, Zerelda Mimms. They had two children, Jesse Jr. and Mary. Zerelda remained loyal to Jesse until his death seven years later.

One of the most famous battles involving members of the James gang was a gun fight in Missouri on March 16, 1874. In this battle John Younger was killed and Jim

Jim Younger

Bob Younger

Frank James

Younger was wounded. A Pinkerton detective and a sheriff were also killed. In September 1876 the gang raided Northfield, Minnesota, in an attempt to rob the First National Bank there. They were clobbered by the citizens of Northfield. Cole, Jim, and Bob Younger were badly wounded and captured. They were sentenced to life in Stillwater prison in Minnesota. When he was being taken away, Cole Younger, with 11 bullets in him, rose and swept off his hat to the watching ladies.

Jesse James was shot to death on the morning of April 3, 1882, in his own home, while he stood on a chair to straighten a picture. His murderer was Bob Ford, a member of his gang, who, with his brother Charlie, had planned Jesse's killing for the $10,000 reward. Frank James turned himself in, stood trial, and was freed. He died in 1915. Bob Younger died of tuberculosis in Stillwater in 1889. Cole and Jim Younger were released in 1901. A year later Jim killed himself over a girl. Cole died in 1916. Bob Ford became a wanderer and outcast. Eleven years after Jesse's death he was killed in his Colorado saloon by a shotgun blast from Ed Kelly, a distant relative of the Youngers.

The inscription on Jesse James's grave reads:

JESSE W. JAMES
Died April 3, 1882.
Aged 34 years six months 28 days.
Murdered by a coward whose name
is not worthy to appear here.

Bob Ford

Billy the Kid

Billy the Kid is second only to Jesse James in the folklore of American outlaws. Because he has been described in so many different ways by so many different people it is hard to say what he was really like. Some writers say he was handsome and daring, others say he was ugly and sneaky. When he was 21 he claimed he had killed 21 men, one man for each year of his life. It is more likely that he killed no fewer than three nor more than 11 men.

Billy the Kid was born Henry McCarty in New York City on November 23, 1859. When he was three he and his parents left New York and went west. By the time he was 14 Billy was living in Silver City, New Mexico, with his mother and stepfather. By the time he was 17 he was hiring out as a gunhand to both sides in a cattle war in Lincoln County, New Mexico. Some stories say that he was already wanted for killing a man in a quarrel. In Lincoln County he used the name William H. Bonney II. He was befriended by an Englishman, John H. Tunstall, an important man in the cattle war, and went to work on Tunstall's ranch.

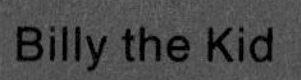

Billy the Kid

Tunstall became the first close friend Billy ever had. Then Tunstall was shot by a posse that favored the other side in the war. Billy swore revenge: "I'll get every son-of-a-b— who helped kill John if it's the last thing I do." And he did it. He shot Tunstall's killers and the sheriff and his deputy as well. Billy, with 14 men, fought out the last battle in the Lincoln County Cattle War, which was ended by federal troops. The house which held Billy and his gang was burned down, but Billy escaped.

The governor of New Mexico, Lew Wallace (who wrote *Ben Hur*), offered Billy a deal. He would give Billy a pardon if Billy would testify against the killers in a murder he had witnessed. Billy turned himself in and testified. He also gave the names of other outlaws. When the time for Billy's trial approached and the governor still hadn't pardoned him, Billy escaped.

He was trailed by Lincoln County sheriff Pat Garrett, one of his old drinking partners, who captured him and put him in the Santa Fe jail. The governor refused to help him, and at the age of 21 Billy the Kid was tried for murder, convicted, and sentenced to hang. Billy thought it was unfair that of all the men who had killed people in

Pat Garrett

the Lincoln County Cattle War he was the only one to be punished. On April 28, 1881, Billy somehow got a gun and killed both his guards. Two months later Pat Garrett tracked him down to a house in Fort Sumner, New Mexico. He hid inside the house when Billy was out, and ambushed him when he returned. Billy died of a bullet wound just above the heart.

Billy the Kid lies buried in Old Fort Sumner with two outlaw friends, Tom O' Folliard and Charlie Bowdre. The stone marker bears the inscription "Pals" and the names and dates. A wire fence protects it from curiosity seekers.

Pat Garrett was shot and killed on a mountain road in a dispute with a tenant rancher. Garrett's grave is unmarked and unfenced.

Joaquin Murieta

Joaquin Murieta

Of all the outlaws who claimed that they were "driven to it," only one group could make the claim truthfully. They were the Mexican outlaws of California in the 1850's.

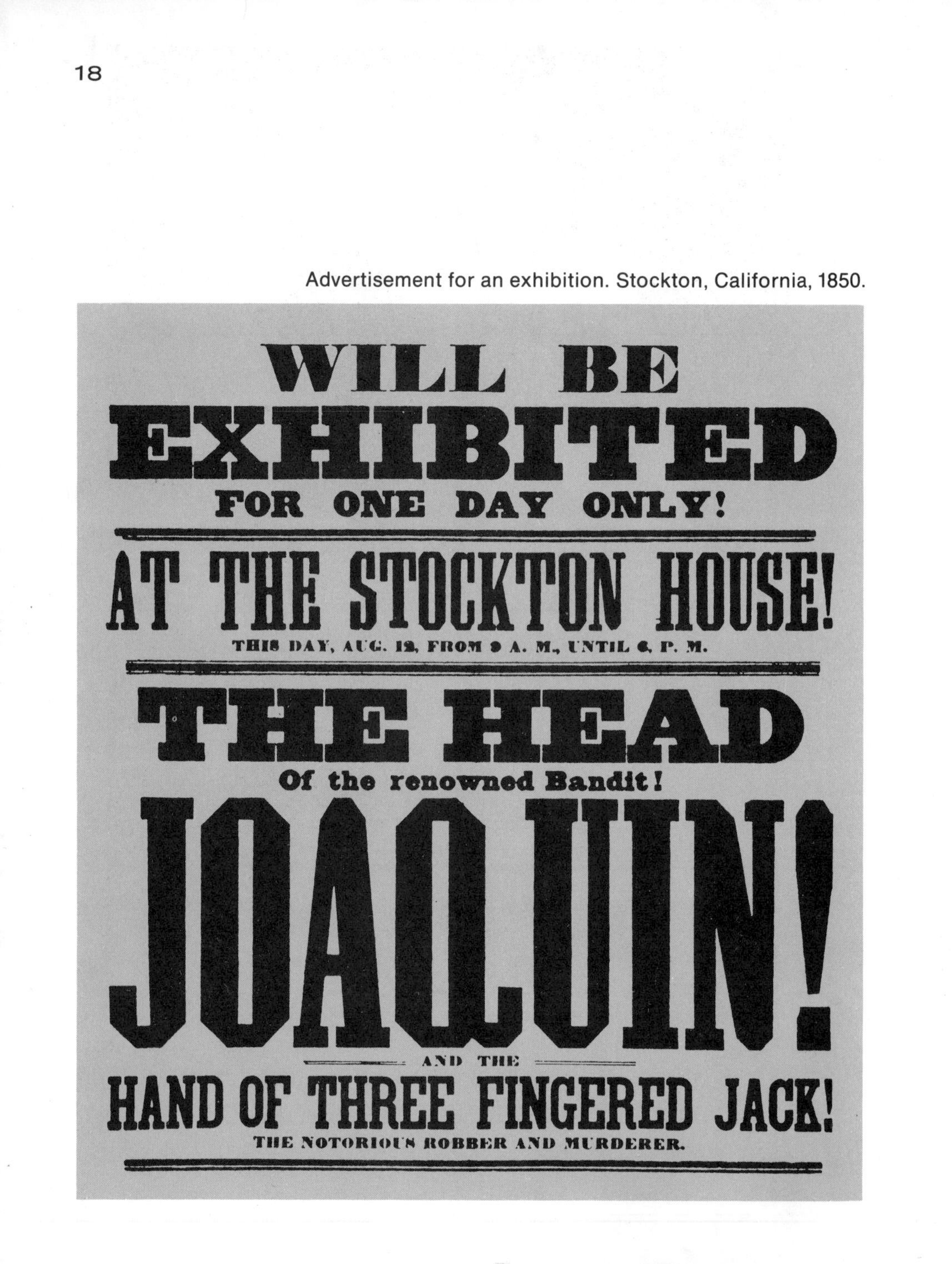

Advertisement for an exhibition. Stockton, California, 1850.

In 1850 the California legislature imposed a tax designed to make it impossible for foreigners to mine gold. This tax was aimed mainly at the Spanish-speaking Americans, some of whom had lived in California all their lives. Bitter Mexican miners formed outlaw bands and began rustling cattle and robbing stagecoaches. There were at least five of these gangs, and each one was said to be led by a man named Joaquin. The governor offered a reward for any Joaquin killed or captured. A group of rangers killed a band of Mexicans sitting around a campfire. Two of the Mexicans were Manuel Garcia and Three-fingered Jack, known outlaws. The rangers did not know the third man. Deciding he must have been a Joaquin, they cut off his head and took it to Sacramento for the reward. Later they obtained papers saying that the head belonged to a Joaquin Murieta, a man wanted for murder. It is still not known for certain whether there really was an outlaw leader named Joaquin Murieta.

The Reno Brothers

There were five of them: Frank, John, Simeon, Clinton, and William. These were the Reno Brothers of Indiana. After the Civil War they organized all the small outlaw gangs of southern Indiana into one big band that controlled the countryside. They committed the first train robbery of them all when in 1866 they held up the Missouri and Ohio Railroad and got away with $10,000. The Pinkertons took off after them and captured John Reno, who was convicted and sentenced to 40 years' hard labor. The rest of the gang carried on the family name. Once Pinkerton captured the entire crew, but they escaped in April 1868. They left a big hole in the cell wall with "April Fool" written over it in chalk. They committed their biggest robbery on Friday, May 22, 1868, when they held up a Jefferson, Missouri, and Indianapolis Railroad train and got $96,000 worth of loot. When Pinkerton learned of their plans to rob another train near Seymour, Indiana, he and his posse hid in the car. They wounded and captured some of the outlaws. Vigilantes seized and lynched five of them.

A few months later William, Simeon, and Frank Reno and four others were arrested in Windsor, Canada, and brought back to jail in New Albany, Indiana. War broke out between the Southern Indiana Vigilantes Committee and the Renos' outlaw friends. The outlaws threatened to get revenge if the Renos were lynched.

On December 11, 1868, masked vigilantes raided the New Albany jail. Frank Reno was dragged from his cell. The noose was tied around his neck and he was hanged to death. Then William Reno was taken from his cell and hanged. Simeon put up a battle, but finally he was knocked out, tied, and hanged. After the vigilantes left, Simeon came to and struggled, jerking and kicking at the air. Slowly he strangled to death.

That was the end of the Reno gang.

Black Bart

Black Bart

I've labored long and hard for bread,
For honor and for riches
But on my corns too long you've tread,
You fine-haired sons of bitches.

Of all the stagecoach robbers, Black Bart was the most romantic. He was a gentleman who conducted his robberies with perfect manners. He was also a poet, and at the scenes of his crimes he often left verses like the one above. His first holdup took place in August 1877. He wore a flour sack with eyeholes over his head, and spoke in a deep, hollow voice. His downfall came when he dropped a handkerchief in making a quick getaway from one of his robberies. The handkerchief was traced to a gentleman named Charles E. Bolton. When he was arrested, Mr. Bolton, alias Black Bart, declared that he had never robbed a passenger or mistreated a human being. After his release from prison, Charles Black Bart Bolton disappeared from the public eye.

Sam Bass, age 16, a boy in Indiana

Sam Bass

Sam Bass, like Jesse James, has been the subject of ballads and legends making him out to be a Robin Hood who stole from the rich and gave to the poor. Sam Bass, like Jesse James, probably did not give to the poor what he stole from the rich. Sam Bass, unlike Jesse James, was not a killer.

Sam Bass, 10 years
later, a Texas outlaw

Sam was born in Indiana in 1851. When he was 10 his mother died. When he was 13 his father died. He went to live with an uncle. At 18 he ran away and went to work in Mississippi for a year. Then he hitched a ride on a wagon train to Texas. In Denton, Texas, he worked for Sheriff William F. Egan until he was fired for getting too involved with horse racing. In partnership with Henry Underwood he acquired a pony named Jenny and traveled around Texas racing her. On one of these trips he met Joel Collins and decided to go up to the Black Hills with him. There the young rovers went broke. They tried to rob a stage, but the stage wouldn't stop for them. When other attempts at stagecoach robbery did not get them much, they decided to try train robbery. They robbed a train in Nebraska and got $60,000, the most loot Sam ever took in one raid. He never again had such luck. He returned to Denton and because of his popularity with the people was able to avoid capture.

But as Jesse James had his Bob Ford, Sam Bass had his Jim Murphy. Murphy, an old friend of Sam's, betrayed him to the Texas Rangers for money. Sam was shot from ambush while casing the bank at Cove Hollow. While he lay dying, the Rangers tried to get the names of his friends from him, but he wouldn't talk.

Sam Bass died at the age of 27. Jim Murphy became an unpopular man, living in fear. About a year later Murphy swallowed some eye medicine and died.

John Wesley Hardin

John Wesley Hardin

J. G. Hardin was a Texas preacher. His son, John Wesley Hardin, was a Texas killer. He was the worst killer in the history of the state. When he was 15 he killed a man who he said attacked him with a stick. In his own life story he claimed to have killed 12 men by the time he was 18.

He spent some time in Abilene, Kansas, where he fought Wild Bill Hickok with words but not with bullets. In the early 1870's he returned to Texas. He killed a few more men, married Jane Bowen, got himself filled with buckshot, was captured and escaped. Then he got involved in a famous feud between two Texas families, the Suttons and the Taylors. He killed a few more men, including a sheriff and a deputy, and became the father of a baby girl.

On May 26, 1874, Wes's 21st birthday, Sheriff Charlie Webb of Brown County, Texas, tracked him to Comanche, where he had settled with his family. He drew on Wes in a saloon and wounded him in the side. Wes killed Charlie Webb and claimed it was his 40th killing. After the killing of Charlie Webb, Wes became a fugitive. A lynch mob hanged his brother and two cousins. Texas Rangers pursued him for three years, until they finally captured him in Florida. He was brought back to trial and sentenced to 25 years' hard labor. When he was released 16 years later, he was 41 years old. His wife was dead and his children grown. He got a pardon from the governor and set up a law office at Gonzales, Texas. Then he started visiting a blond named Mrs. McRose, the wife of a cattle rustler. When McRose was killed, Wes claimed he had arranged

Old John Selman

the killing. Later he had to make a public apology to the killers, who didn't care to share the credit.

Next, Wes insulted Young John Selman, a policeman who had thrown Mrs. McRose into jail for vagrancy. Selman's father, Old John, didn't like the insults. On the night of August 19, 1895, Old John entered the Acme Saloon. Wes was shaking dice with the bartender for drinks. Old John Selman shot him in the back of the head. He died.

The following April Old John was shot in what his killer described as a gun duel. No gun was found on his body.

Belle Starr with Blue Duck

Belle Starr

Belle Starr, queen of the horse thieves, was born Myra Belle Shirley, February 5, 1848, in a Missouri log cabin. Her father came from an aristocratic Virginia family. At the age of eight she became a pupil at Carthage Female Academy. When the Kansas-Missouri border war broke out, the family moved to Texas. In Texas, Belle met Cole Younger, who, with his brothers, was hiding out after a Missouri bank robbery. She fell for him.

Then Belle, with her baby Pearl, met Jim Reed. She fell for him too. They fled to California because the law was on Jim's trail. In 1869 Belle and Jim, with two other outlaws, stole $30,000 in gold from an old Indian. Jim and Belle returned to Texas with their share of the loot and the children, Pearl Younger and Edward Reed. In Texas Belle became known for wearing a velvet gown, shiny boots, and six-shooters, and riding a black mare.

Belle Starr

When Reed was killed, Belle left the children with her mother and devoted her full time to her career. From 1875 to 1880 she was the leader of a band of cattle and horse thieves in Oklahoma. She met an Indian named Blue Duck and fell for him. Then she met another Indian, a Cherokee named Sam Starr, and fell for him. She and Sam married and settled on a piece of land owned by Sam. She named their place Younger's Bend.

In 1883 Belle was tried for horsethieving and sentenced to six months in the federal prison in Detroit. Sam was sentenced for a year. When they were released they returned to Younger's Bend. In 1884 Belle took part in a Wild West show, but she soon returned to her first love, stealing horses. In 1886 Belle and Sam were arrested by U. S. marshals, but the charges were dismissed for lack of evidence.

Sam's end came when he was killed by a dying Indian deputy he had shot. In 1889 Belle was killed by a bushwacker on a lonely road.

REWARD
$10,000
IN GOLD COIN
Will be paid by the U. S. Government
for the apprehension
DEAD OR ALIVE
of
SAM and BELLE STARR
Wanted for Robbery, Murder, Treason
and other acts against the peace
and dignity of the U. S.
THOMAS CRAIL
Major, 8th Missouri Cavalry, Commanding

The Daltons

The Dalton brothers of Oklahoma were cousins of the Younger brothers, who rode with Jesse James. There were 15 children in the Dalton family. Three of them, Bob, Grat, and Emmett, rode together as outlaws. A fourth, Bill, became an outlaw later. The Daltons' heydey covered a period of 18 months in the early 1890's. Bob and Grat were in their twenties, Emmett not yet 21. Their first big escapade was their robbery of the Santa Fe Railroad's Texas Express in 1891, which got them $14,000. From that time the Dalton name was feared in the Southwest. Their scouting was done by Eugenia Moore, Bob Dalton's sweetheart, who got information about the trains and scouted the railroad depots. Emmett Dalton was in love with pretty Julia Johnson, but he felt it was unfair to ask her to marry an outlaw. The patient Julia waited.

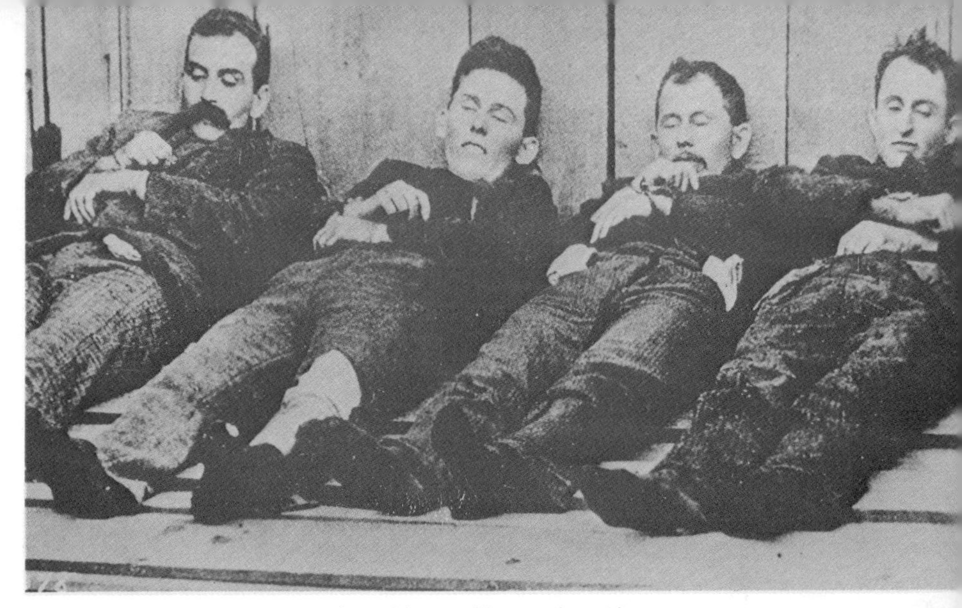

The Dalton gang, shortly after death:
Bill Powers, Bob Dalton, Grat Dalton, and Dick Broadwell

(left) Bob Dalton and Eugenia Moore

The end of the Dalton gang came when they raided Coffeyville, on the border of Oklahoma and Kansas. Bob and Grat were killed, and Emmett was filled with 18 buckshot. Near death, Emmett rallied and recovered, with Julia and his mother, Adeline Younger Dalton, at his bedside. In 1893 he was sentenced to a life term in the Kansas State Penitentiary. In 1907 he was pardoned and released. He came out a reformed man and married the waiting Julia. They settled in Los Angeles, where Emmett Dalton became a building contractor, real estate man, and movie writer, and often declared that crime does not pay. He died July 13, 1937.

Bill Doolin

Bill Doolin of Oklahoma started as a member of the Dalton Gang. On the way to Coffeyville, his horse went lame and he had to turn back. It is suspected that common sense rather than his horse's lameness might have caused him to turn back.

Bill Doolin was a likable, fairminded killer. He once refused to let one of his men shoot Marshal Bill Tilghman in the back. The Doolin Gang's favorite hideout was the town of Ingalls. On September 1, 1893, a posse of marshals rode into Ingalls, and after a bloody battle, the gang was driven out. From then on Bill was pursued by Bill Tilghman.

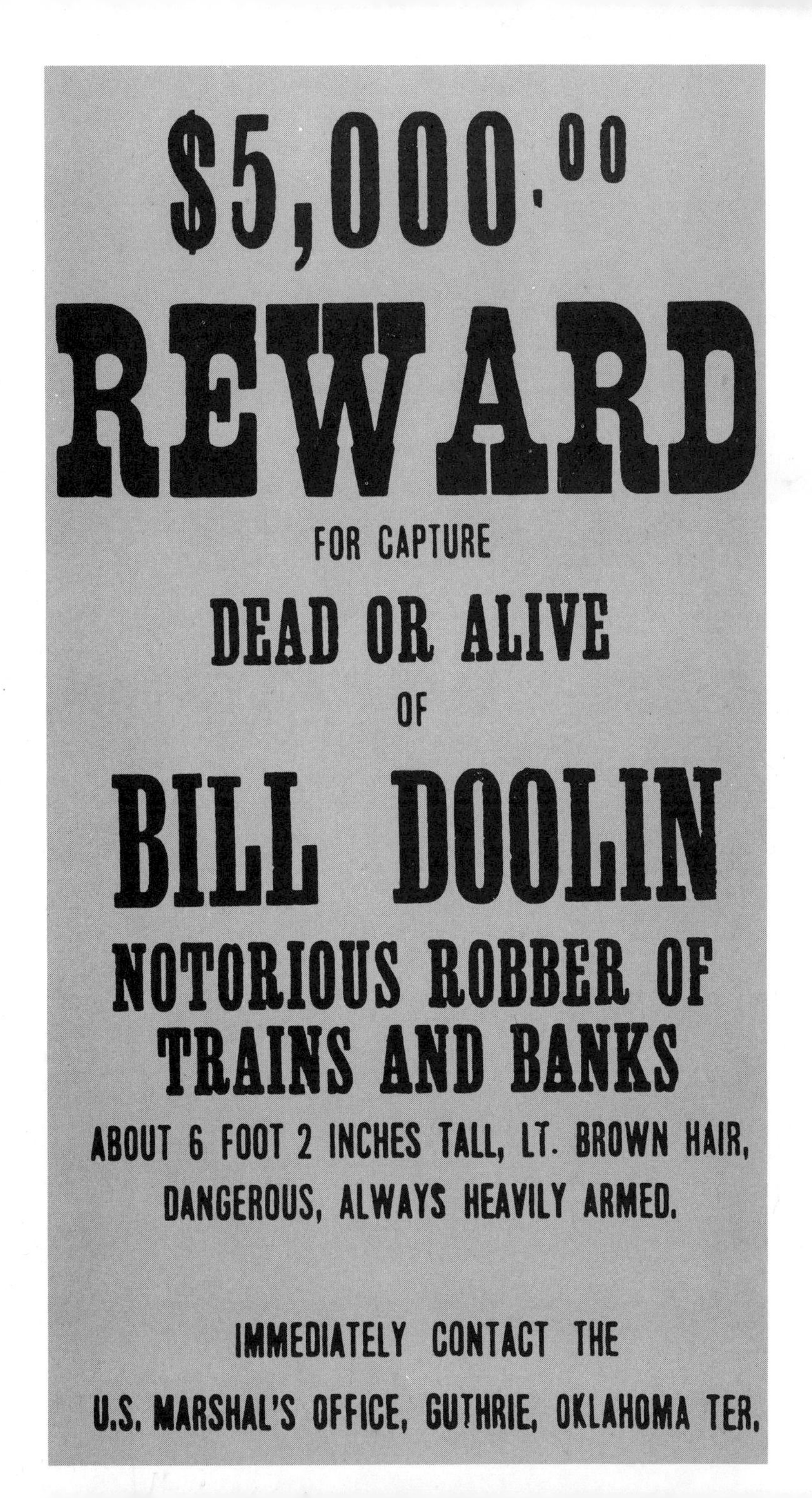
$5,000.00
REWARD
FOR CAPTURE
DEAD OR ALIVE
OF
BILL DOOLIN
NOTORIOUS ROBBER OF
TRAINS AND BANKS
ABOUT 6 FOOT 2 INCHES TALL, LT. BROWN HAIR,
DANGEROUS, ALWAYS HEAVILY ARMED.
IMMEDIATELY CONTACT THE
U.S. MARSHAL'S OFFICE, GUTHRIE, OKLAHOMA TER.

Rose of Cimarron was not formally charged with committing a crime. Marshal Bill Tilghman, always fair-minded, protected her by releasing this photo of another young woman, possibly Jennie Metcalf.

One incident in the battle of Ingalls has been repeated so many times that it has already become a legend. A beautiful woman known as "Rose of the Cimarron" was in love with "Bitter Creek" George Newcombe of the Doolin gang. When Bitter Creek lay wounded in the street, Rose ran out to him. While Doolin and the gang held off the marshals, Rose dragged her lover to safety.

In 1894 Bill Doolin married a minister's daughter and robbed a few more banks and trains. In about 1896 Tilghman finally captured him at Eureka Springs, Arkansas, while he was taking a hot bath. When Tilghman took him in, people crowded around to cheer Bill Doolin.

While he was being held for trial, Bill escaped from the jail, freeing 37 other prisoners. He returned to his wife and child, apparently ready to settle down to a law-abiding life. One night, when Bill Doolin was walking down a lonely road, leading his horse and followed by his wife driving a wagon, Marshal Heck Thomas shot and killed him.

Bill Cook

While Bill Doolin was attracting attention in western Oklahoma, the lesser known Bill Cook was breaking records in eastern Oklahoma. In three months' time the Cook gang pulled off 10 stagecoach, store, bank, and railroad holdups. This was a record. During all these holdups only one man was killed. This was also a record.

Bill Cook was born in 1873. He was orphaned in his early teens. At 14 he ran away from the orphanage and began drifting from ranch to ranch as a cowboy and farmhand. Because of his liking for whiskey he needed more money. He got it by bootlegging liquor to the Indians. He was jailed twice, and it seemed as if the second jailing had straightened him out. But then his brother Jim got into trouble with the law and ran away, and Bill joined him. The Cook gang was born. On July 14, 1894, the Cooks robbed their first stage. On July 16 they robbed their first train. Two weeks later they robbed their first bank. And so they continued taking in loot and riding high, pursued by Heck Thomas and the Indian police. They entertained themselves by writing messages and jokes on the reward posters put out for them.

Bill Cook

When it got hot in Oklahoma and some of Bill's men were taken in, he fled to Texas. When it got hot in Texas, he fled to New Mexico. In New Mexico Bill Cook was tracked down and finally captured in Billy-the-Kid country, near Fort Sumner.

Cherokee Bill

Crawford Goldsby, better known as Cherokee Bill, was actually only one-eighth Cherokee. He was also part white, part Mexican, part Sioux, and part Negro. Crawford was born in Fort Concho, Texas, on February 8, 1876. His brother Clarence was born two years later. His mother sent him to an Indian school at Cherokee, Kansas, and later to the Carlisle School for Indian Youths in Pennsylvania. After two years at Carlisle, he returned home and moved in with his mother and stepfather.

He soon began to get into trouble. When he was 18 he shot a young Negro and, mistakenly thinking he had killed him, ran away, took the name Cherokee Bill, and joined the Cook gang. He was now a husky, broadshouldered young man of great physical strength. He killed a man in the Cooks' first bank robbery, and then broke away from the gang to go it alone.

During his outlaw career he killed between seven and 13 men, including a railroad conductor who had asked him to pay his fare or get off the train. He also killed his sister's husband, George Brown, because he wanted some of George's hogs.

Cherokee Bill was captured through his sweetheart, Maggie Glass. Deputy W. C. Smith paid Ike Rogers to invite Maggie to spend a few days with Ike and his wife, who was Maggie's aunt. Cherokee Bill hurried over to visit Maggie. On the second day, Mrs. Rogers sent Maggie to a neighbor's on an errand. While she was gone, Ike and his friend Clint Scales hit the outlaw on the head with a piece of firewood, and, after a long, hard struggle, got him down to the floor and handcuffed him. They took him in to the law. Ike's treachery made him unpopular, especially with Cherokee Bill's brother, Clarence Goldsby, who shot him in the neck, killing him.

Cherokee Bill's trial was long and drawn out. The outlaw's mother obtained a well-known lawyer, J. Warren Reed, to defend her son. The trial developed into a contest between Reed and Judge Isaac Parker, the hanging judge. Cherokee Bill was sentenced to hang, but the execution was postponed because Reed appealed to the Supreme Court, claiming that the trial had been unfair. While waiting for a ruling from the Supreme Court, Cherokee Bill killed a guard in an attempted jailbreak. He went on trial again and was sentenced to hang. In the meantime the Supreme Court supported the verdict in the first trial.

At his hanging, Cherokee Bill was asked if he had anything to say. "Hell, no," he replied. "I came here to die, not to make a speech."

The Apache Kid (center) served as a government scout in the campaign against Geronimo, 1882.

The Apache Kid

At the age of 20, the Apache Kid, following Indian law, killed a man who had murdered his father. With a small band of friends he became a fugitive from white man's law. Two years later he turned himself in and was granted a pardon. But he was convicted and sentenced for

The Apache Kid (center) and his friends, before their trial.

killing a whiskey salesman on the reservation. The Kid and his band escaped and went on a rampage of robbery and killing that spread fear throughout Arizona. It ended suddenly in 1894. Some authorities say that the Kid probably got across the border into Mexico and stayed there.

Annie Rogers and Harvey Logan

The Wild Bunch

The Wild Bunch, the largest and most organized of all outlaw gangs, operated in the 1890's over an area that included Wyoming, Utah, and Colorado. Among its most famous members were Butch Cassidy, Kid Curry, the Sundance Kid, and lady outlaw Etta Place. The Bunch was actually an army of several outlaw bands. It was outlawry's last stand, as pursued and hunted outlaws banded together for survival and mutual protection.

Top man of the Bunch was Robert Leroy Parker, known as Butch Cassidy. He took his name from a childhood idol, outlaw Mike Cassidy, who taught him rustling and gunfighting. From 1890 to 1892 Butch was a wandering cowhand. Then he began a career that followed the familiar trail from rustling to bank holdups and express robberies. By 1897 he was the undisputed leader of the outcasts. Though he was an expert marksman, there is no evidence that he killed anyone until the last battle for his life in South America.

The Wild Bunch's number-one killer was Harvey "Kid Curry" Logan. Kid Curry was a quiet, reserved, gentlemanly murderer who is known to have killed at least eight men. At the age of 19, Logan, with his brothers Lonny and Johnny, left home to become a cowboy. He joined a gang of rustlers and went on to bigger and better things. He named himself Curry after a rustler, Flat Nose George Curry, whom he admired. His career is spotted with vicious, cold-blooded killings.

The Bunch's last train robbery took place on July 3, 1901. They robbed a Great Northern train at Malta, Montana, and took in $40,000. Then they fled to Texas. There Butch took up bicycle riding and could be seen biking around the red-light district of Fort Worth. Kid Curry separated from the others. He was captured in Knoxville, Tennessee, and convicted, but he escaped from the Knoxville jail. He went to Colorado and organized a gang. On

The Wild Bunch. Seated: Harry Longbaugh, Ben Kilpatrick, and Butch Cassidy. Standing: Bill Carver and Harvey Logan.

Etta Place

July 7, 1903, Kid Curry was killed in a gunfight with the law.

Butch Cassidy, Sundance Kid, and Etta Place went to New York and had a blast in the big city. From there they set sail for South America. Butch and Sundance went to work at the Concordia Tin Mine in Bolivia and introduced outlawry to the Pampas. Etta returned to the states for an appendicitis operation and stayed. Butch and Sundance died in 1908 in a gunfight with the Bolivian cavalry after a mine holdup.

the author

Frank Surge is a native of Buhl, Minnesota. He attended the University of Minnesota, where he received a B.S. in English and an M.A. in Education. He has taught high school English for several years in Minnesota and Illinois, and now works in the Publications Division of the Minnesota Department of Education. He lives in St. Paul.

The Pull Ahead Books

AMERICA'S FIRST LADIES
1789 to 1865

AMERICA'S FIRST LADIES
1865 to the Present Day

FAMOUS SPIES

SINGERS OF THE BLUES

WESTERN LAWMEN

WESTERN OUTLAWS

We specialize in publishing quality books for young people. For a complete list please write

LERNER PUBLICATIONS COMPANY

241 First Avenue North, Minneapolis, Minnesota 55401